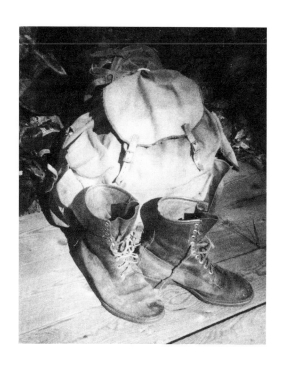

Green Mountain Adventure,

AN ILLUSTRATED HISTORY, BY

Vermont's LONG TRAIL

JANE & WILL CURTIS AND FRANK LIEBERMAN

THE GREEN MOUNTAIN CLUB, *Montpelier, Vermont, 1985*

A Curtis-Lieberman Book

Copyright © 1985 by The Green Mountain Club
Library of Congress Catalog Number 85-80828
Softcover ISBN 0-930985-02-8
Hardcover ISBN 0-930985-03-6
The text of *Green Mountain Adventure*,
Vermont's Long Trail
was set in Trump Medieval
with captions and marginals in Palatino italic,
and printed by Whitman Press, Lebanon, N.H.
on Mountie Matte by Northwest Paper Co.
It was bound by New Hampshire Bindery, Concord, Mass.

Design and typography by Frank Lieberman

On the title page, sunrise from Camel's Hump, 1935. GMC

Acknowledgements

The authors especially wish to thank Green Mountain Club members Bob Attenborough, Ray Catozzi, Smith Edwards, Corky Magoon, John Nuffort, John Paulson, Shirley Strong, Don Wallace and John Willey for the help they gave to make this book possible. Field supervisor Ben Davis and Harry Peet, Executive Director of the Green Mountain Club, freely gave their time and graciously overlooked our disruptive presence in Club headquarters. Louis Borie, Mary Fenn and Alice Delong also contributed generously to the book, as did the Cecil Howard Charitable Trust.

Katherine Shepard, librarian at Vermont Academy, Connell Gallagher, archivist, Bailey-Howe Library, were most helpful while Reidun Nuquist, Green Mountain Club member, far exceeded her duties as librarian for the Vermont Historical Society by reading "Green Mountain Adventure" manuscript. Emma Hunt of Charlestown, N.H., reminisced about her teacher and friend, James Taylor, giving lively glimpses of the founder of the Green Mountain Club. And lastly, "Green Mountain Adventure" would have never come to be without the invaluable encouragement and help of Green Mountain Club President, Preston Bristow.

For the use of the photographs that illustrate this book we are most grateful. Each source is credited by means of small initials in the picture captions: —

B H L   The Bailey-Howe Library, University of Vermont, Burlington

G M C   The Green Mountain Club, Montpelier, Vermont

P P M   Priscilla Perry Merritt, Bloomfield, Connecticut

J P   John Paulson, Bennington, Vermont

M F   Mary Fenn, Brownsville, Vermont

V H S   The Vermont Historical Society Library, Montpelier, Vermont

On the side of Stratton Mountain James Taylor conceived the idea for the Long Trail. VHS

The Long Trail

James Taylor sat in his forester's tent on the side of
Stratton Mountain and looked out at the summit
through the unceasing July rain. There were no trails
to the top and it was too wet to bushwack. But for
Taylor it was fine just to sit and think about the past
year. School was over; on the whole it had gone well;
the class of 1909 had been a bright bunch of boys and
girls; he had enjoyed teaching them. There had been
satisfaction too in his job as Assistant Headmaster of
Vermont Academy in the little town of Saxtons River. It might not be a big school but, by golly, it had
a big campus. "The Grand Campus" he liked to call
it, stretching from Mt. Ascutney in Vermont to Mas-
sachusett's Greylock. Being Assistant Head meant
that he could institute some ideas close to his heart.
The closest being his desire to get the boys on campus out into the countryside. What was the point of
living in one of the most beautiful states in the Union
and never getting to know its beauties at close hand?
He hated to see them wasting their time sitting about
indoors. Much better to get their legs working climbing mountains, getting oxygen into their brains. Their
health would certainly improve and even perhaps
their grades! Well, he'd led boys up neighboring
mountains now for several years and they liked the
expeditions better every year. The school had even
accepted his idea of getting credit for a mountain
climb, A for Ascutney, G for Greylock.

The trouble was there were so few mountains
with connecting trails although there were mountains
all about. Of course there was good old Mt. Ascutney,
the boys' favorite. They loved hiking up the carriage
road and sleeping on the top in the stout granite hut.
Part of the fun of climbing Ascutney was knowing

At the turn of the century climbing Killington was not easy! For the less adventurous, however, there was a carriage road to Killington Mountain House. VHS

that the mountain was among the first in America to boast a hiking trail. Windsor folk, hoping to give aged General Lafayette a thrill, cut a footpath on the mountain in 1825 as a first step in making a carriage road up which the hero could ride in style. Alas, history doesn't say if the grand ascent was ever made!

There had been that disastrous trip up Killington a year ago. There was a trail of sorts, the Mountain Road, but it was in terrible shape, washed out where it wasn't overgrown. The boys' idea of carrying a large pail filled with fresh asparagus and water caused a good deal of trouble, sore hands and sloshed water, but they insisted they wanted it for a sumptuous breakfast on top. The accommodations were a disappointment, nothing but the collapsing kitchen ell of the ruined Killington Mountain House. They had made the best of that of course but the night was calamitous: — all through the dark hours whole tribes of porcupines came out to gnaw the ancient grease of the kitchen floor, squealing and scrabbling about without let up in spite of yells and flung boots. Sunrise revealed further casualties; an overturned kettle, and mangled asparagus stalks strewn about Killington's rocky summit. But boys are tough creatures, little sleep and no breakfast faded before the prospect

of an exciting hike across the range from Killington to Pico. That had been the final blow! There was simply no trail across the range from Killington to Pico! And no time to make a bushwacking trip. He could still hear their mournful refrain as they returned to Saxtons River, "No go to Pico!"

James Paddock Taylor ran his hand through his thick black hair, a gesture he knew amused his pupils; it caused him to resemble a large porcupine. There was no use of talking about the Grand Campus and good health and wild beauties if no one could get into the wilderness to see them.

He looked out at Stratton's summit, a fine mountain but again, no trails. The Germans, now they had the right idea. He'd enjoyed every step of the walk he'd taken a few years ago on the Black Forest hiking trail. Why couldn't there be such a trail on New England's mountains? Why not?

The rest of that rainy day James Taylor sat and ruminated on a vision of a trail linking the summits of Killington and Pico, linking Mansfield's Chin and the Lake of the Clouds; maybe even a trail running from the Massachusetts line to the Quebec border along the tops of the Green Mountains! And why not some shelters along the way like those in the Alps?

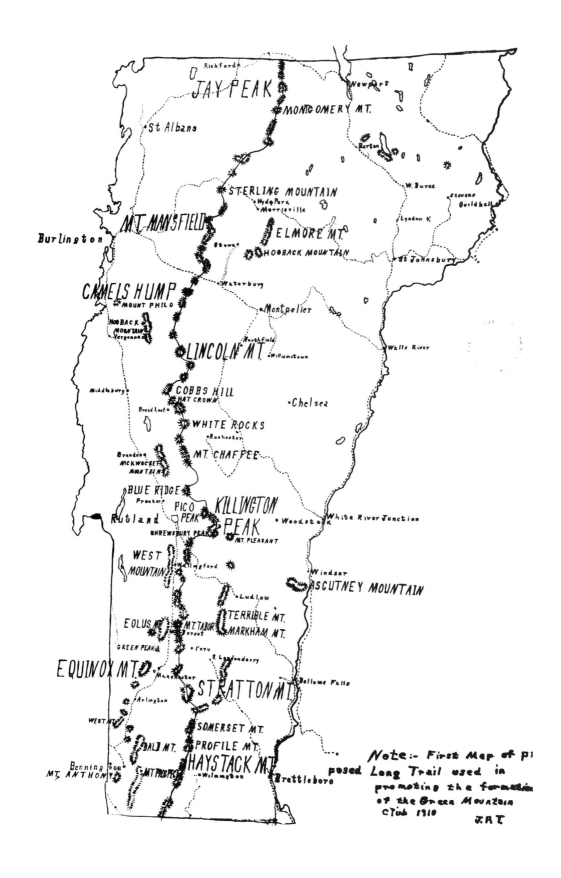

Note:- First Map of proposed Long Trail used in promoting the formation of the Green Mountain Club 1910
J.R.T

That, history has it, was the way the idea of the Long Trail came about in the fertile mind of James Paddock Taylor, and of an organization to maintain such a trail, the Green Mountain Club. To bring about both took a lot of doing, but James Taylor was nothing if not a magnetic, vital individual with imagination, energy and great powers of persuasiveness. Emma Hunt of Charlestown, N.H., pupil and friend of James Taylor says, "Jimmy was a man who could make things happen!"

After his rainy day in the tent he sketched out a rough map of a foot trail along the top of the Green Mountains and took his idea and his map to ask advice of the venerable Appalachian Mountain Club in Boston. But for the Appies there was only one mountain range, the White, and Taylor claimed they believed "The Green Mountain state was as flat as a pancake!" It was plain that any attempt to bring his dream to life would have to be done in Vermont by Vermonters.

For a year at every meeting he attended, for every influential man he met, he brought out his map. He had an interview with the Governor who listened to the persuasive teacher, looked at his map and gave his approval. So did the state forester, a college president and a brace of lawyers. But Taylor knew that in order to get anything as ambitious as a mountain pathway there must be a flood of information if the people of Vermont were to entertain the notion that it would be "fun" to walk on their mountains. For years the ancient peaks were considered nothing but a hindrance to easy communication across the state.

Even when the fashion of mountain-top hotels had been at its height, Vermonters regarded those who walked or rode up a carriage road as tourists who might be crazy enough to do anything. Hard-working folk had too much to do to want to walk up a mountain. It was Taylor's dream to change this attitude.

In the early part of 1910, Taylor had gathered enough support to consider establishing an organization to oversee the building and maintenance of his dream mountain pathway. On March 11, 1910 at 2 p.m., twenty-three Vermonters met at the Van Ness House in Burlington to form the Green Mountain Club. The infant organization's only asset was $100

James P. Taylor, founder of the Green Mountain Club. GMC

Opposite; Taylor's much-used map of his proposed Long Trail over the Green Mountains. VHS

James P. Taylor, Saxtons River, Vt.
M.E. Wheeler, Rutland Vt
Frank H Clark, Windsor, Vt
[C.B.] Hollister, Barre, Vt.
[W. Thomas] Stowe Vt.
[ ] Houlton, Burlington, Vt.
[ ] Angell, Hartford, Vt.
[Carroll] H. Brown, Wallingford, Vt.
[Arthur W.] Eddy, Bristol, Vt.
Frank E. Sawyer, Vergennes, Vt.
[C.] H. Brownell, Burlington
[ ] Southwick
[ ] Whitehill, [Fairlee] Vt
[F.] R.B. Flint, Northfield Vt.
[J.] E. Tracy, Burlington
[W.] Chittenden, Burlington
[Horace] J. Brown, Montpelier
[Clarence] P. Cowles, Burlington
Edward H. Allen
[C.] H. Morrill, Randolph
D. T. Page, Bakersfield
[C.W.] Gates, Franklin, Vt

Signatures of the twenty-three who met in Burlington to found the Green Mountain Club on March 11th, 1910. *BHL*

from Mr. M. E. Wheeler of Rutland. The stated purpose of the Club, "Shall be to make the Vermont mountains play a larger role in the life of the people." Naturally James Taylor was made its first president.

The charter members were a distinguished group of Vermonters; lawyers, editors, judges, school principals, professors, men who were leaders in the state. In fact it was later said that in order to make any mark in the state of Vermont it was necessary to belong to the Green Mountain Club!

The first governing body, beside the usual officers, was a council, consisting of a member from each county, which was supposed to cut trails, build shelters, issue maps and guidebooks. But it was quickly realized that these objectives could not be carried out with such scattered control. The idea of a "Section" was a natural one. Why not organize a chapter in the area through which the trail would pass, to be responsible for a part of the trail? Thus the Sections came into being, almost independent clubs, whose devotion to the idea of the trail and whose hard work in maintaining it has given the Long Trail its reputation as one of the best in the continent. Burlington Section has the honor of being the oldest, started in August 1910 and known then as the Mt. Mansfield Section, and proud to boast that among its ninety-five members, there were even some women! Bread Loaf came along in 1911, then Brandon and Rutland, while Bennington was organized in 1914.

After the momentous meeting in the Van Ness House members could hardly wait for the snow to melt from the mountain sides. "When do we chop?" they asked. Mt. Mansfield would be the logical place to start, two Burlington enthusiasts agreed. So, with axes in hand Judge Clarence Cowles and Craig O. Burt started the huge task of cutting a trail from Mans-

A 1927 post card view of the famous Mt. Mansfield House, showing the Carriage Road, bottom, right. GMC

field's Chin south to Nebraska Notch. It was only three miles but it was a start.

Excitement spread to other regions of the state. "A small party of women are desirous of climbing Mt. Mansfield if that is at all possible," wrote Miss C. M. Whitcher of Passumpsic to James Taylor, asking for information.

President James Taylor knew that Vermonters wouldn't take the trail and the club seriously until they could see that a walkable path had been made from one peak to another. What could be more noticeable than a trail between Mansfield and Camel's Hump, Vermont's two most prominent mountains? As soon as the school year ended in 1910, Taylor armed with his axe and a huge ball of string and one helper, set off for Mansfield vowing to blaze as much trail as he could in his two weeks of vacation.

He managed to mark a trail from where Cowles and Burt had left off, towards the Winooski River, indicating where he thought it should go, then crossed the river and started a trail towards Camel's Hump, for others to finish. There were plenty of willing members who could see that indeed there would be a trail between Mansfield and Camel's Hump.

The year 1910 saw the beginning of the Long Trail

James Taylor's next tasks would be to make the name of the Green Mountain Club and its Long Trail a familiar one, to get permission from landowners over whose land he had planned a path on his map and most important of all, gain members. If the notion of a trail 265 miles long seemed formidable, Taylor never let on. Tirelessly he travelled about the state talking to any person or group that would listen, unfolding his now much-creased map for the hundredth time. Sometimes his audience responded in a jocular manner to his address as when the aged landowner and legislator, Hap Hapgood, the "Inker of Peru," faced with the question of how to cut a trail over Bromley Mountain, replied, "Let the women do it!" Another landowner of vast acreage over whose mountain Taylor hoped to run the trail, was Joseph Battell. At a meeting that had allotted three hours to a discussion of the Long Trail's route, Battell spent 165 minutes expounding on the corpuscular theory of sound! In the final fifteen minutes Battell said yes, the trail could go over his Mt. Lincoln.

Taylor got all the publicity he could ask for when the *Vermonter Magazine*, then the most popular publication in the state, devoted an entire issue to the Trail and the Green Mountains. In the May, 1911 issue, member Louis Paris told the people of Vermont that the Long Trail would bring into the state new ideas, encourage better roads, services, higher standards of living, new markets for produce and would only cost five cents a mile! Before the summer of 1911 was out, Paris boasted the club would have in use thirty miles of trail from Sterling Pond to Camel's Hump, across Smuggler's Notch, Mt. Mansfield, and Bolton Mountain!

That was the summer when Judge Seneca Hazelton laid a trail from the summit of Mt. Mansfield to Smuggler's Notch, when the logging roads on the north side of Camel's Hump were used to make a through trail from Bolton to an old trail to the summit of Camel's Hump. It was the summer when Taylor put up signs and blazed trees and cleared the route of that trail, to make it the first portion of the Long Trail to be put into service.

Mt. Mansfield, some forty years ago, with the Winooski River in the foreground. VHS

15

But although James P. Taylor is the father of the Long Trail, Dr. Louis Paris deserves an equal amount of credit for organizing not only the early trail building but keeping the Green Mountain Club alive during the first years while serving as Secretary, Chairman of Membership, and Treasurer.

In addition to persuading landowners to let the trail pass through their property, there was the task of organizing sections to cut and maintain the trail. Louis Paris wrote Taylor in 1911 that now Rutland and Brandon Sections (presently Killington and Bread Loaf Sections) had joined the Club, "We must not hold too many offices in Burlington, though it is certainly convenient." His comment clearly underlines the difficulties of maintaining contact in preautomobile age and at a time when few had telephones! And then there was the problem of finances. Paris despaired, "The treasury is low, not one section except here (Mansfield) has submitted the 25%. The treasury of Mansfield is minus nil. The Trail over Bolton Mountain to Mount Mansfield has proved a costly job. Thoroughly well done and good for years, but it cost more than we had in the treasury."

Difficulties with finances and communication notwithstanding, the work went on and by the end of 1912, the trail could be followed from Camel's Hump to Sterling Pond, thanks to Fred Mould who had worked north from Smuggler's Notch. For Taylor who was sitting dreaming in his tent only three years ago this was immensely gratifying, but he and the other trail builders knew what enormous efforts of labor and time still had to be expended before the Trail was in reality the "Long Trail." The Club was weak in membership, funds and knowledge; its only asset was the members' enthusiasm. So when the State Forestry Department came to the Trustees in 1912 with the idea of constructing a fire patrol trail through the mountains, it seemed like an answer to a prayer. Would the Club's interest be served by this fire trail? It would take the burden of construction from the members' shoulders. The State proposed to provide the labor if the Club could come up with money. In spite of the low level in the treasury it was voted to go ahead with the agreement. It was a decision to be bitterly regretted a few years later.

Major Jenks, left, and Louis Puffer on the Trail from Boyce. GMC

Opposite; The highest cliff in Smuggler's Notch. An 1897 photograph, long before the road was paved. PPM

With $475.00 from its own funds, the Club gathered in $100.00 generously donated by the Appalachian Mountain Club, another $100 from the ever-helpful Proctor family and $25 from the Woodstock Inn, even then a mecca for outdoor enthusiasts. Finally the Club was able to raise $1,065, the sum estimated necessary by the Forestry Department.

All was well at first. The State woodsmen commenced working in 1913, northward from Killington towards Brandon while another party chopped their way from Camel's Hump to Lincoln Gap, finishing their work in a remarkably short time. By August the State had cleared the entire distance from Killington to Camel's Hump. Fifty miles had been added to the trail in one summer! What is more there was the exciting discovery of a cave "near the Woodstock Road at the height of land," (now Route 4 at Sherburne Pass). Dr. Paris with an eye for the dramatic decided it should be named "Deer Leap Cave."

A dedicatory hike was announced to celebrate the accomplishment on August 17th. Fifty people turned up to walk the 6 miles from Killington Peak to Sherburne pass. There was more to celebrate. The pro-

Sterling Pond in the mid-20s. GMC

prietor of the Woodstock Inn paid to have a side trail cut during the summer from West Bridgewater to the top of Killington. Bennington had been working hard too, and had completed the trail from the Massachusetts line to the summit of Stratton Mountain and to a point two miles east of Manchester. At the same time the Sterling Section had cut the trail north so that it could be followed from Sterling Pond to Johnson, only fifty miles from the Canadian Border.

The members were just congratulating themselves on the remarkable feat of providing over a hundred miles of mountain walking when reports came in that the trail from Killington to Brandon was a disaster! "I was over parts of the trail shortly after its completion and for miles it was impossible to follow the path . . . even with the guidance of one of the foresters who had helped build the trail, in a day's hike of 14 hours we were lost a half dozen times," said Will Monroe. The State Foresters had underestimated the amount of money needed and in order to get the job completed had done little more than blaze trees and clear the worst of the slash and fallen trees.

Even worse was the fact that in order to speed up the work the men had followed old logging roads along the lower slopes of the mountains and made no attempt to climb along the crest of the chain. Louis Paris said that the trail passed through burned-over valleys and sections that had been heavily logged while Allen Chamberlain in his "Vacation Tramps in New England Highlands" wrote that "Unfortunately, the necessities of the forest patrol did not fully harmonize with the ideals of the tramper. A route across the ridges was too meandering and laborious to meet the foresters' needs and the trail that they ran on easy grades . . . was far too tame and unspectacular for those whose quest was scenery."

The Club Trustees were horrified. What they had on their hands was a disaster; why would anyone wish to get into the woods only to stumble over slash far below the summits?

But that was just the point said the Forestry Department, we want a fire trail with a good easy grade of fifteen percent up which fire equipment can be dragged. Roderic Olzendam, Club Corresponding

At times it was a bit difficult to find the best route for the Long Trail. BHL

19

Secretary and defender of the Forestry Department's point of view said, "A small number of enthusiastic men laid out the first trail but the Long Trail is to be for women also."

In the southern part of the state Bennington had laid out their section of the trail in the same fashion, using existing logging roads in order to have a completed pathway in the quickest possible time. Their hearts were in the right place but under the leadership of Lawrence Griswold and Wills Wright the trail was later relocated to more interesting areas.

Members commenced to take sides, the stalwarts darkly suspecting that the Forestry Department wanted the fifteen percent grade so they could ride burros on the trail. "This is not the West!" trumpeted the stalwarts.

It did not help matters when the then Lt. Governor of Vermont put his oar in with the suggestion that the Long Trail go straight through the middle of towns. Louis Puffer didn't like that idea at all!

Into the midst of the conflict erupted Professor Will Monroe, one of the most dynamic in the Club's cast of characters. John Willey, Camel's Hump historian, calls Will Monroe, ". . . a colorful and irascible man with a powerful personality." A teacher at the New Jersey State Normal School and expert in Balkan Languages, Monroe first came to Vermont in the summer of 1914 to teach at the University of Vermont. He discovered the Green Mountains and in particular Camel's Hump, which he came to regard as his own private mountain. He even insisted that it be called "Couching Lion," a name which on flimsy evidence he claimed was that of discoverer Samuel de Champlain.

Monroe joined the club, hiked over the trail and found it so badly overgrown and indistinctly marked that it was not safe to follow. When he offered to organize and pay for a trail building unit, the Trustees asked him to work south from Camel's Hump. Eventually the crew with Will Monroe relocated the trail as far south as Middlebury Gap. That was fine, but Will complained to Roderic Olzendam and then to President Proctor about the terrible job the Forestry Department had done. He neatly sliced open a hornet's nest. Both Olzendam and Proctor were in

Two early pioneers of the Bennington Section. Irving Hare and Wills Wright in the Hagar Clearing. JP

favor of the Department, particularly as Austin Hawes, Chairman of the Trails and Shelters, was also Commissioner of the Department and Proctor's classmate at Yale.

Olzendam and Hawes were angry at Monroe. He should have, they scolded, complained to the Forestry Department and not embarrassed them by writing to the officials of the Club since it was the Forestry Department's trail. Theron Dean, boon trail-cutting companion, cautioned Monroe that Vermonters hated outsiders criticizing their affairs and that too much complaining might alienate the generous Proctor

An early view of Camel's Hump from the east. VHS

21

family. That didn't stop Monroe, he went right on telling everyone about his work on the new and very superior trail he had engineered, the "Skyline Trail," as he called it, to contrast with the dismal affair of the Foresters down among the stumps.

Years later Aston Allis, part of the Will Monroe trail-building party, remembered the ox team and Farmer Callahan looking like an ancient patriach driving a two-wheeled cart with a week's camping supplies up to a pretty little place the Professor called, "Montclair Glen." Monroe, it was said, "named everything, every rock, bump, tree and blade of grass." Today most of the forty mile section of Monroe's Skyline Trail is the route taken by the present Long Trail. The story of Will Monroe's association with the Callahan Farm comes in a little later, but his demand that he be allowed to form a New York Section nearly cleft the Green Mountain Club in twain! By this time Monroe had made himself thoroughly disliked by many in the Club and for those who were in sympathy with the objectives of the Forestry Department, Will Monroe's demand was the last straw. Monroe had, in the summers he'd relocated the trail, collected about him a goodly number of vigorous folks from New Jersey and New York who were eager to join the Club as a section.

The New York Section on a hike up Camel's Hump in 1920. Will Monroe is seated third from left. GMC

Russin Rock Refuge. GMC

People from New York and New Jersey joining the Green Mountain Club? The Club was for Vermonters. Didn't the Club Constitution say so? The out-of-staters should be content with the status of "guests." At that Will Monroe's temper began to rise alarmingly (after all the work he'd done!); What DID the Constitution say, Monroe demanded!

Where was it? No-one had any idea. It was most embarrassing. Theron Dean was, "greatly mortified to learn there is evidently no copy of our present constitution in existence!" There was nothing to do but to locate an old copy of Dr. Louis Paris' *Vermonter* of May, 1911. There, it was found that article 5 stated that members of the Club in any district of the State might organize a section. Taylor pointed out it didn't mean an out-of-state section couldn't be accepted.

23

Trail work on the southern face of Camel's Hump, from one of Theron Dean's hand-colored glass slides. BHL

President Proctor became alarmed over the uproar and asked that a conference between the representatives of the New Yorkers and the Club be arranged, "In order," he said, "that the entire organization might come to some firm, friendly and satisfactory decision in the matter . . ." Cowles, Taylor, Woodruff and Dean agreed that the offending article must be amended to include a section of the New Yorkers. Will Monroe, maker of the Skyline

Trail, and his cohorts could not be relegated to the status of "guests."

Writing to Monroe after the annual meeting in January, 1917, Dean said that the article had been taken care of and also the prickly question of the fifteen percent grade. He almost lost his temper, he wrote, when Olzendam got up once more to urge the easy route but that James Taylor had risen to his feet and in a most tactful speech said that the policy of the Club was to create in the Long Trail, ". . . a high, scenic, mountain pathway." There it was; Taylor had expressed in a few words what the lovers of the Green Mountains had wanted to bring about. Ever since then the Green Mountain Club has tried to maintain the Long Trail in accordance with those words.

The way was clear, too, for the creation of out-of-state sections, even an out-of-the-country section, the Montreal Section. Under Will Monroe's aegis, the New York Section started off with a bang, 148 members at the first annual meeting! Such a vigorous organization needed focus for its energy and two camps were built for the section's use, Wyanoki Lodge in Northern New Jersey and in 1922, Thendara in New York's Interstate Park. Today the New York Section is still, over sixty years later, a vigorous, enthusiastic part of the Club, testimony to Will Monroe's spirit and still caring for the portion of the trail he loved.

With those problems out of the way the Club could get down to achieving a more efficient use of labor and money. The Trustees had learned their lesson. "We must have a very systematic scheme," said President Proctor, "for the location and building of the trail . . . Then whatever section we work on this summer or any other summer will be a definite part of the trail system and there will be no danger of duplication of our money and endeavors."

It made sense to first put in order the trail between Smuggler's Notch and Camel's Hump. The section between Lincoln and Killington should be next on the books and when that was done the gap between Lincoln and Camel's Hump should be addressed. Attention could then be turned to the trail between Killington and Manchester. Last would come the final push from Smuggler's Notch to Canada.

"there should be a very systematic scheme for the location and building of the Long Trail."

25

With renewed sense of dedication, Middlebury Section in 1917 built Pleiad Lake Lodge, while C.P. Cooper and Willis Ross planned and built much of the trail south from Killington to Prospect Rock.

Necessity, it is said, is the mother of invention, and the men who spent their summer vacations maintaining trails already cut and making new sections had to have adequate tools. One ingenious member devised a combination hoe-rake for clearing trash and making waterbars, a tool adopted by many of the sections, but Will Monroe's 4-foot cross-cut saw was less popular. "Remember how some of the helpers grumbled over carrying that saw last summer?"

Once the trail was blazed and cut the question of an adequate method of sign posting had to be solved. What color paint for marking the trail over rocky summits? Advice from the experts at the Appalachian Mountain Club was to "use white, yellow or blue but never red which soon turns dark and cannot be seen." Others from the Boston club didn't agree at all. The Green Mountain Club's own James Taylor thought that white was best in his opinion and that the whole trail should be marked with white blazes and signs. No, said the Bennington Section, they liked red markers and they didn't care that some of the upstart New York Section got lost and complained about the poor job of marking that the Bennington Section had done. They said that a number of Appies had come through and had complimented them on their visible signs! They were using a four-inch disc nailed to a tree in the center. However, it was found that as the tree grew bark around the disc, it was turned into a funnel.

The Club experimented with a larger disc, say six inches, one side turned up. Nailed in with two nails and projecting from the side of the tree it could be seen from either side thus saving from having to use two discs. But then, said Dean, "every fool hunter" would use it as a target. Mrs. Dean, said her husband, had instructions to save all can bottoms so that tests could be made. More sophisticated were the experiments with tin arrows and triangles, painted red, white, blue, and yellow, nailed to members' trees and observed in differing lights and season. In the end Taylor's suggestion was adopted and the entire Long

No one could agree on what color should be used to mark the Trail!

Trail is now blazed with white for the main trail, blue for side trails.

Although during the war years action was slowed, the cry was "Killington to the Massachusetts Line!" By 1917 that goal had been achieved and at the October meeting in 1919 it was estimated that in a few more weekends the Long Trail would be located from Johnson to the Line with only thirty miles left to complete it northward to the Canadian Border.

That the trail had been almost finished in only seven years was due in great part to the "Mountain Saints" as Taylor called them. Their names still resound along the ravines and slopes of the Green Mountains; Judge Clarence Cowles who went out in March 1910 to start work on Mt. Mansfield; C.P. Cooper, painter of signs whose paint-spattered jacket was known the length of the trail; Elihu Taft, Theron Dean, Professor Will Monroe, Willis Ross, Louis Puffer, and Mortimer Proctor, giver of the Long Trail Lodge, now alas only a happy memory. The Club has over the years made a practice of keeping green the memories of their devoted members by naming shelters, camps, lodges, lookouts, and even mountains after them. Ever since the early days women

The Vermont-
Massachusetts line,
Nov. 10th, 1934. PPM

27

have worked just as devotedly and been memorialized in recognition of their service to the Club and for their love of the Mountains; today, shelters are named for Lula Tye, Minerva Hinchey, Laura Woodward, and Emily Proctor.

Now that the trail was almost complete an adequate guide book must be issued. Back in 1911 Louis Paris hoped that the individual sections would see that their guides were printed in uniform size so that all could be bound together as the Green Mountain Club's official guide to the Long Trail. In 1917 the Club issued a guide in three sections with maps, each describing a part of the trail. The northern part, called the Mt. Mansfield guide, went from Johnson over Mt. Abraham to Lincoln Gap. South of that, in section two, conditions were poor; only the trail from Mt. Carmel to Killington was described in this manner:

"Since preparing copy and maps for the Guide Book, C.P. Cooper and W. M. Ross of Rutland have been over the trail from Sherburne Pass to Mt. Carmel, 8 m. north on the Long Trail from Killington to Mt. Horrid (Rochester Pass on the Brandon-Rochester road) and report it in excellent condition

JOHNSON R'T & J.E.C.R.R.

To Jeffersonville

Morse's Mill
Morse's Mt.
B. Scully's
Whiteface
White Rocks
Mould's Shelter
Beaver Meadow

MANS

STERLING

Lake of the Clouds

CHIN

Madonna

TO
MORRISVILLE

TO
UNDERHILL
CTR.

Hotel
NOSE

Sterling
Pond
Barnes Camp

FOREHEAD

Smugglers Notch

New
Forestry
Trail

Trout Club

TO
STOWE

Nebraska Notch

Sugar
Loaf

Lake
Mansfield

TO
MOSCOW

Bolton Mt.

Camp

BOLTON

C.V.R.R.

Honey Hollow Trail
to Jonesville

Farm

Winooski
River

STENDS

Randall Camp

TO NO. DUXBURY AND
WATERBURY

CAMELS
HUMP

Camels Hump Club

HUMP

Callahans

Huntington
Trail to
Richmond

Bakers Notch

Montclair Glen

Ira Allen

Burnt Rock

TO
RICHMOND

To North Fayston

Bean's
Farm

Birch Lodge
Beaver
Meadow Camp

Molly Stark

Baby Stark

Applach'n Pass

Stark Pass

Genl. Stark

Glen Ellen

Ellen Mt.

TO
NEW HAVEN

Lincoln Mt.

Mt. Abraham

Davis

The Long Trail
The Johnson–Lincoln Mt
Region
Scale 5½ Miles to Inch.
(Approximate)
▪▪▪▪ The Long Trail
• • • • • Supplementary Trail

and well marked. The Brandon Section had promised to clear and mark the trail from Carmel to Mt. Horrid as early as this season as possible, but it is probable trail is in fairly good condition now. The Long Trail to Horrid runs north along west side of Mt. Carmel through low point of Wetmore Gap, west by north to and around west side of Bloodroot Mt., thence north across brook. Following brook west leads to Barber's Steam Saw Mill near junction of brook and Furnace River where lodging and food usually may be secured and egress made to Pittsford or Brandon on the Rutland RR.''

To the south, one could find information about the Stratton Mountain Trail from Prospect Rock, east of Manchester, to the road below Sucker Pond. Seven hundred members were listed with their addresses, the Sections mentioned at that time were Brandon, Burlington, Bennington, Ryegate, Putney, Stowe, and New York. Much of the book was concerned in that pre-automobile age on simply getting to the trailhead. Here is how one might approach Stratton Mountain in 1917: ''Take West River Railroad from Brattleboro north to Londonderry. Leave railroad at Wardsboro Station, take auto stage to Wardsboro and then on to

West Wardsboro. In this village there is a good country hotel, the Green Mountain House. Full directions for climbing Stratton Mountain may be obtained here.''

This skimpy attempt at an official guide book was far from what Paris had in mind but the difficulties under which members tried to get accurate measurements were trying, to say the least: laboriously done with a measuring wheel. ''From the kitchen on the summit of Camel's Hump to the fireplace at the bend of Callahan Trail south of cliffs, 1.2 miles: fireplace to junction of Callahan to fork on ox road, 1.4 miles,'' read one set of calculations. The next book, issued in 1920, assumed the form it has today and directions read from south to north, which seems to be the most natural way. Since then it has gone through twenty editions.

Transportation took a great deal of planning in those days before the automobile. Letters of the time have pages of elaborate schedules involving trains, horses and wagons and occasional car. Just getting Will Monroe back to New York City on a Sunday night took some doing. A car would take him from Moody's via Lincoln Center to New Haven Junction where he could get a sleeper at 10:30 but he had to

In the pre-automobile age horse and wagon transported hikers to the head of the Trail. BHL

be sure to get on the New York car which lay over until 1:05 when it would be hitched onto the New York train and arrive in the city in the morning. A jaunt by the Burlington Section in 1916 sounded like this: "The plan is to go to North Duxbury on the early train — Eaton's autos to Callahan's, Skyline Trail to just south of Burnt Rock Mt. and from Slash Rock down that ravine or valley to the east — SUPPOSED(!) to bring the party out at North Fayston saw mill by 5 p.m. and auto from there to Waterbury to catch the 6:45 train due in Burlington at 7:40 p.m."

To illustrate how important the railroads were then, when the club was incorporated in 1917, Rutland was chosen as headquarters because the city was so well connected with the rail system.

By the '30's the Club was advising bus travel as a way to get to the trailhead but even as early as 1921 the shape of things to come were made plain by President C. P. Cooper's request. He wanted the sections to put up highway signs on the main road crossings so that the trail would be noticed by passing cars. He would himself paint and mark them for he considered they would be good advertising for the club. He later said it was more of a job than he'd looked for, but that ten years later all the signs were still standing on their creosoted posts.

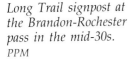

Long Trail signpost at the Brandon-Rochester pass in the mid-30s.
PPM

32

If the routing and cutting of the trail was the Club's first priority, building a chain of shelters was the next. James Taylor sitting in his tent that first day on Stratton Mountain had in mind something like the refugios of the Alps, a system of mountain huts spaced for a day's hike apart. Miss Emily Proctor had given $500 in 1914 for that purpose and three shelters were built using that money that same year, one at Birch Glen, one on the Lincoln Ridge, and one just south of the Brandon-Rochester Gap. Will Monroe's Skyline Trail boasted Montclair Glen Lodge, also one of the earliest shelters on the Long Trail. But the hiker of the early days had to depend on abandoned lumber camps and farm houses of obliging hill farmers whose places lay near the trail. For years Mrs. Frank Beane of Hanksville was a legend among knowledgable hikers for her hospitality and helpfulness in every way dear to hiking tribes' hearts, from transportation to relaying messages. The Mt. Mansfield Hotel was a mecca for years until that grand old lady was torn down in 1964. Near the top of Camel's Hump the huts of the Camel's Hump Club provided food and lodging. By 1917 the first edition of the Long Trail Guide advised that a hiker could find 14 shelters along the way including private camps, old lumber camps,

Hanksville was a convenient place to pick up mail and supplies. GMC

33

Long Trail shelters
came in a variety of
sizes and materials
and provided equally
varied accommodation;
few were luxurious.

*Opposite; Griffith
Lake shelter near
Dorset. GMC Porky
Lodge, Killington. MF
Fred Tucker Camp,
Hazen's Notch. GMC
This page; Abandoned
Gates Camp. PPM
Theron Dean Shelter,
GMC Cauchnawaga
Shelter, Bennington
Section. GMC*

Until it was razed in 1964 the Mt. Mansfield House was quite literally the high point of many a summer visitor's holiday in Vermont. BHL

the Mt. Mansfield Hotel and five Green Mountain Club shelters. In addition, those who wished to hike off the trail could find nine nearby farmhouses willing to take in boarders.

By 1920 when the second edition of the guide came out the Club could boast of nine more shelters with an additional twelve farms located near the trail. At that time the Green Mountain Club could look proudly on its accomplishments, 209 miles of trail, 14 shelters built by the Club, and a membership of 800. Two years later in the Club newsletter the *Green Mountain News* (later changed to *Long Trail News*) it boasted that three new cabins had been built that year, one on White Face, one on the Bondville Road, and one between Styles Peak and Bromley. "All are equipped with bunks and stoves."

Three camps were acquired with ease when the venerable Camel's Hump Club turned over its property near the summit in 1922, the only proviso being that members be able to use the camps and their eighteen heavy wool blankets free of charge.

Shelter building wasn't easy. "There may be a time," said one hard working volunteer, "when airplane landing stations can be hewn out of mountain sides, as things are now the work of preparation is enormous. The site has to be chosen with care and, regardless of how inaccessible this may be, the axes and saws, hammers and spikes, chains and shovels and all the other tools, all have to be lugged up on the backs of men . . ."

Then the Club was faced with another problem, upkeep of its property. Already by 1917 the original Emily Proctor Shelter was in need of repair. Since then many of the original shelters have been replaced and many have been renamed. The oldest existing shelter is Taft Lodge on Mt. Mansfield, given by Elihu

Taft Lodge, winter. GMC

Taft in 1920. It is also the largest, as befits Vermont's tallest mountain, accommodating thirty-two. Governor Clement Shelter in Shrewsbury built in 1929 is another veteran. Ritterbush near the end of the trail, built in 1933 and maintained by the St. Albans Section, still offers shelter at the end of a day.

The now-vanished Fay Fuller camp in Bennington's section, made of stone, was the only shelter designed by an architect, Paul Thayer, architect for the Long Trail Lodge.

For years the Club had no official clubhouse and perhaps felt like a poor country cousin when Appie Alfred Hurd wrote to say that he'd like to come to "Call at the Green Mountain Club Rooms." "Now think of that!" said Theron Dean, "We haven't even got a headquarters!" But by 1917 the Club had itself incorporated and had decided its headquarters should be centrally located in Rutland.

In 1922 came the exciting news that a clubhouse was assured and would be built the next year at Sherburne Pass where the trail crossed the highway. President Mortimer Proctor telegraphed from Los Angeles to Acting-President Cooper, "I wish to donate complete the new Green Mountain Club House to be built near Deer Leap on Sherburne Pass."

With his mother, Mrs. F. P. Proctor, he generously gave the land and money to build what was long considered to be the home of the Green Mountain Club. Set among the woods at the top of the Pass it was built in the "rustic" style. Visitors never forgot their amazement when they entered the lobby whose walls weren't wood and plaster but a huge fern-covered rock ledge down which trickled a miniature waterfall. The club was particularly pleased with the effect of the dining room. The architect had left bark

40

on the yellow birch beams and had designed a great
chandelier of ten lights made of white birchlimbs
with shades of birch bark. In addition the Lodge had
a resident naturalist, Maurice Braun, who set up on
the grounds around the lodge what was probably the
first self-guided nature walk in the state. The most
astonishing feature of the Lodge was that the Long
Trail went right through the building!

Glad as the Club was that it had at last its own
clubhouse, it soon became apparent that operating the
lodge only as a clubhouse was too much for the Club
to carry alone. Paying guests were the answer and to
accommodate them, cabins were added in hopes that
a profit could be made. That hope never materialized.

Three interiors of the Long Trail Lodge; the living room, a corner of the dining room and the massive stone fireplace in the living room. All GMC

41

Some trail problems seemed to persist for years; crossing the Winooski River was one. In 1912, $500 was appropriated by the legislature for a bridge at Bolton, but the Town of Bolton refused to undertake its upkeep and the money was never spent. In 1922 the Club provided for a ferry and ferry man to row hikers across the river. The arrangement was less than satisfactory as evidenced by this account: "Crossing the river at Bolton is certainly interesting. On our trip last summer the only time I was scared of my life was when we got into the old flat-bottomed boat and were rowed over by a farmer woman to the Bolton side. The boat was half full of water when we arrived and our entire party tipped it over and drained it out. When the farmer woman, who was rather stout, got in to row us across she said the only thing the matter with the boat was that the bottom was weak and as the current was rather strong at that point, I fully expected to go through the bottom all the way across and was certainly a happy man when I put my foot on the further shore."

The ferry crossing of the Winooski was uncomfortable, at best. Passengers had to bail if they wanted to keep their boots dry. BHL

When the question of a bridge at Bolton came up again in 1926, somehow the Legislature's money had disappeared. Next year, in the great flood of 1927, the

Club's boat was swept away, the only real damage the Club sustained that catastrophic fall. In 1935 the guidebook advised that, "a ferry, .25¢, is run by the Bert May family whose house is at the left of the trail on the road near the south bank of the river."

For another twenty-nine years one boat or another ferried hikers across the Winooski until 1964 it was decided a more reliable method of crossing was necessary. The portion of the old Skyline Trail that followed the ridge down to the river, is now called the Bamforth Ridge Trail and is designated a side trail. Don Wallace laid out the new part that leads to the Jonesville Bridge, a safer but tamer crossing than by the old ferry boats.

As the Green Mountain Club was a home-grown organization, so in the early days was its administration. In the absence of any paid directors or secretaries, the officers handled all duties, inquiries, correspondence, publishing guide books, issuing maps, hiring caretakers, overseeing upkeep of trails and shelters. In the days before easy telephone communication, almost all correspondence was by letter and much of it hand written at that. The office of Corresponding Secretary carried with it a heavy burden

A warm day on the Trail from Little Rock Pond to the Griffith Job in the Wallingford area, 1936. GMC

once the Long Trail commenced to get publicity. Inquiries as to trail conditions and lodging had to be answered by busy men who had their own affairs to tend to, but to attend to questions they did. Club archives are filled with long letters meticulously answering not only the questions but describing views, advising on prices of transportaion and where to get a train or bus. Some of the letters were like this from a Mr. Lewis: "I would like to take a motor trip through the mountains and wish to know the conditions on the trail and also on the Lion's Claw Trail." James Taylor, Corresponding Secretary, wrote back, ". . . that neither the grade or its surface or its width permit auto traffic." Was Mr. Lewis anticipating by ten years the proposed Green Mountain Parkway?

There were other problems. Some one had to deal with hikers who wrote complaining that the heavy ferns on the trail between Montclair Glen and Bolton

Lodge were getting their legs wet in the morning. Or with the suggestion that the Long Trail be patrolled along its entire length every two days and watchmen be employed to check lodges and camps every 48 hours to prevent thefts. (Even in those far-off days vandalism was a problem. The lodge on Lincoln Mountain, wrote Will Monroe, should be moved, ". . . its location on the line of hike of hoodlums from the towns of Bristol and Lincoln made it an undesirable site.")

Then there was someone who thought that the name of the Long Trail should be changed to that of the Green Mountain Trail, ". . . since it is not now the longest trail, the Appalachian Trail is." The Club retorted that the Long Trail's name was well established and besides, it was the longest state trail!

There were complaints that the trail food available at the Long Trail Lodge was too heavy. There should be larger supplies of boullion cubes, hard chocolate, and "tiny tins of sausage and compact nuts."

Finally the work load got to be too much for these dedicated officers. Volunteers, faithful and hardworking as they all were, they couldn't be expected to carry on in a business-like manner the affairs of an increasingly complex organization. Miss Lula Tye took over the office of Corresponding Secretary in 1926 under the old arrangement but in 1932 it was plain that the position demanded a salary. The Trustees voted to pay her $250 a year; and when the next year she assumed her duties of treasurer she received $375 a year.

Lula Tye saw to it that the affairs of the Long Trail ran smoothly and she did so for twenty-nine years! When she retired in 1955 another devoted member of the Green Mountain Club took her place, Minerva Hinchey. Under her management the club came by its well-known address of 108 Merchants Row, Rutland. Fred Field, Green Mountain Club member, whose secretary was Minerva Hinchey, generously allowed the club to use his office as its business address. Minerva Hinchey faithfully served the club until she retired in 1977 at the age of eighty-two. It was the next year that the office was moved to Montpelier.

Lula Tye, who faithfully served the Club as Secretary and Treasurer for almost thirty years. Succeeding her was Minerva Hinchey, who gave the Club twenty-two years of devoted service. GMC

45

For the men who had spent a vigorous summer cutting trail and erecting camps in inaccessible spots fall and winter provided a new challenge. Some of the hardier souls responded by climbing the mountains on snowshoes. Some went up the summer carriage roads such as those on Killington and Mansfield, others were more adventurous. On February 21, 1920, H. W. Congdon, Leroy Little, and C. P. Cowles climbed up to the chin on Mt. Mansfield, down the steep pitch to Hell Brook and Smuggler's Notch to make the first winter ascent of Vermont's highest mountain. From then on C. P. Cowles was never happier than on his midwinter adventures. He would ride the train to Bristol, hire a sleigh and man to take him to the last farm house below where the present McCullough highway crosses the range. He would camp overnight on top of the ridge, then slog down to Birch Glen and on to Huntington Center. His equipment and clothing were minimal by today's sophisticated standards. He would find a large boulder, pitch his open-faced tent facing it four or five feet away, build a fire between the boulder and his tent, then snuggle down into his wool quilted blankets on a bed of spruce boughs.

Miss Guthrie, left, who shortly fell into a deep snowy hole. BHL

"I used smallish snowshoes, bear paws, made by the same man who made Peary's, Dunham I think his name was. I wore a wool union suit, sweater, business coat with collar turned up, cap with ear flaps, wool socks, and mittens. Cold or blizzard never stopped me . . . to keep warm I simply kept going vigorously."

Soon a small group of men and women were pioneering in what later were called "winter sports." At times the going wasn't as easy for long-skirted females as it was for Clarence Cowles. "Coming down the northerly side of the Forehead, Miss Guthrie stepped on top of a balsam covered with snow, the branches gave way under Miss Guthrie's weight and engulfed her to the armpits. Dean and I took off one of our snow shoes and dug Miss Guthrie out of her predicament." Unperturbed, Miss Guthrie struggled on down the trail, her long skirts plastered with snow.

Clothing in the early days, evidenced by Cowles' winter outfit, wasn't a case of displaying one's status but of simply being comfortable. The recommended equipment for the hiker in 1916 consisted of "ordinary height shoes with hobnails, felt hat, 'generous-

Members of the Burlington Section on a Washington's Birthday outing at Taylor Lodge, February 22, 1927. James Taylor is fifth from right, front row. GMC

Expedition to Killington Peak, March 1916. GMC

Hardy souls enjoyed winter camping, sensible folk preferred shelters. BHL

sized' silk bandana, inch wide leather belt with cup attached, wool underwear, wool shirt and stout wool trousers.'' Female hikers should have high laced boots with ''Hungarian Nails'' and wear bloomers. But, it was cautioned, it was just not done for ladies to be seen on city streets in this costume. In the early 20's some of the keener female minds had devised a way for getting around this taboo by having tailored breeches made with fitted jackets and a cover-up skirt to hide the horrid sight of a woman in a hiking outfit. In this way they were able to conceal the offending masculinity until the trailhead could be reached.

Both sexes were cautioned to keep their money and railroad tickets in a rubber tobacco pouch, carry a whistle for signalling and have available a rubber officer's cape. Two woolen blankets with safety pins laid on a waterproof silk ground sheet would make for a comfortable night but be sure to bring a long handled axe, naptha soap for washing woolens and a carbide lamp with extra carbide in a moisture-proof tin. One wonders whether there was any room for food left in the Adirondack pack baskets common in

Crossing Black Brook near the Grout Job, 1920. JP

those days. "As for food avoid carrying supplies with large amounts of water, look into the possibility of using dehydrated potatoes, milks, and soups. To off-set the digestive effect of concentrated foods, carry along some dried fruits. Cheese and macaroni and baked beans are staple trail foods." Hikers were told to bring a coffee pot and frying pan with a tin cup and plate and a canvas water bucket, plus two pails that nest. But don't carry all this in a blanket roll across the chest! Use a pack basket or an army knapsack.

One reason for the increased number of those using the Long Trail was Theron Dean's lantern slide show. Dean had become a good photographer and over the years managed to cover the length of the Long Trail, clambering about with his heavy camera and precious glass plates. This was his own enterprise, entailing some difficulties, chiefly the problem of getting the colorist not to tint the rocks too red, "Remember this is not the West!" To cover his travelling expenses and his not-inconsiderable photo-

A foggy day in June.
GMC

51

graphic costs, he had to charge a fee of $35 plus a night's lodging, for this was before the era of easy transportation. The shows were extremely popular. Between February 7th and 27th, for instance, Dean gave eleven shows all over the state to an average group of eighty-eight people. Such were the days before TV! John Paulson of the Bennington Section remembers going with his father to hear Theron Dean and seeing the large carbide-lit projector that got very hot indeed, and remained so for an hour. He was told not to touch it and still remembers the burn on his forefinger!

Such was the fame of the slide show that a mountaineering group in California wanted Dean to ship the glassplates to the West Coast, but Dean said he was ''. . . exceedingly attached to the collection and there might be little accidents happen to them. . .'' By the early 30's the Club had taken possession of the glass slides and was still showing them. But by

Miss Jackson on the root of a dead tree well-known to hikers of the day. Camel's Hump in the background. From Theron Dean's slide collection. BHL

52

that time there were complaints that really the show should be brought up to date. One little boy shown hiking with his father had grown up and had two little boys of his own on the trail! In the mid-forties Green Mountain member and photographer John Vondell was asking for kodachrome slides in order to put together a new show. With the passage of time the second show in its turn has been replaced.

In 1926 the Long Trail received a good deal of unsolicited publicity which the Club soon wished would just go away. It did, but it took a while since it was caused by increasing numbers of fast-speed hikers racing up and down the Trail, trying to outdo one another and get themselves in the news.

It all started with one Irving D. Appleby of Roxbury, Massachusetts. Appleby, reported the *Long Trail News*, had hiked the entire Long Trail at one go! (this was four years before the trail was completed to the Canadian Border.) He had gone from Jay Peak to the Massachusetts line and claimed he had hiked the 256 miles in 14 days and 5 hours. "A record we think will stand for some time if not forever!"

James Taylor was ecstatic. It was just what he'd been looking for, "A good chance to get something for the Associated Press." He envisioned a Mountain Marathon which would put the Long Trail on the map, "Where hiker after hiker tries to better the record already made!"

In 1927 Appleby was back in the *Long Trail News*, claiming he'd beaten his first record, this time going north, and what is more he'd carried his exhausted companion's pack from the Dufresne Job to the Manchester-Peru highway. At that some of the experienced old-timers began to have a few doubts. Appleby said in that case he'd do it a third time with a camera man following him. Perhaps the camera man wasn't able to keep up with the swift Mr. Appleby; in any case, the results were inconclusive. The Trustees demanded to see his itinerary; Appleby was outraged. In the meantime, Boston papers had heard of his exploits as Taylor had wished; Appleby was headline news. Store windows in Boston exhibited his trail clothes, sweat-stained shirt, battered pack and the worn boots. (Appleby didn't wear the then fashionable leather puttees, he claimed they prevented his

. . .but the Green Mountain Club was not interested in speed records

53

Irving Appleby in his Long Trail hiking outfit. A 1927 newspaper photograph. GMC Below; The Three Musketeers who travelled the length of the Trail in 27 days. BHL

leg muscles from having full play.) Crowds of college youths gathered about the store windows vowing to better Appleby's time or die in the attempt.

While the boys were getting ready for the trail, three girls who came to be known as the Three Musketeers traversed the entire trail in 27 days of actual hiking and were given a heroines' dinner in North Troy. Newspaper attention switched to them. The *Long Trail News* printed an account of their trip and Appleby, now known as the Baron Munchausen of the Long Trail, was miffed. They were young and pretty females, he said, that was why the Trustees hadn't asked to see their itinerary. There still exists a rather good newspaper photograph of Mr. Appleby, clad in his famous hiking costume, carrying a banner on which the word "Green' can be made out.

There was a perfect flood of hikers' asking advice and help from the Club by those who were planning to race along the trail, while claims of faster and more extraordinary feats of hiking the Long Trail came into Headquarters. It was too much; in April, 1928 the Club approved a resolution stating that the Green Mountain Club wasn't interested in speed records.

The Beardsley family on Killington in 1931. MF

The Long Trail was for the "release and relief from hurry and confusion prevalent in modern life."

Appleby and those who raced after him were hiking the trail for the wrong reasons but they inadvertently began what has now turned into the 'End-To-End", hiking the trail in a summer or a lifetime. No competition here, no records, no medals as Appleby wanted, simply the memories of unforgettable days in the mountains. The hiker has only to present to club headquarters a written summary of the trip (or trips) in order to receive a certificate and the right to sew on one's pack the emblem, "End to End."

In the late twenties groups of all-women hiking parties were taking to the trail in ever greater

The result of porcupines at work on the outhouse at Whiteface Shelter.
GMC

numbers, ". . . to share with menfolk the thrill and uplift of the skyline ridges." In 1929 Miss Edith Esterbrook of Boston led such a group, "all good sports," she said. It was well that they were, for the girls had to deal with a porcupine causing an "ominous gnawing" by deftly hitting it on the nose and boiling it in the cook-pot for an hour. Miss Esterbrook reported that his liver resembled the nicest calf's liver.

In 1934 two Vermont girls, the Misses Pelsue and Urie, hiking the trail from north to south, were a bit more bloodthirsty; they equipped themselves with a pair of .32 Colt automatic pistols, ". . . carried chiefly as a means of killing porcupines or any other pest that sought our company too persistently." It is not reported what the other pests may have been but they said that they disposed of at least a dozen porcupines.

Females were making their way onto the Board of Trustees as well. Miss Esterbrook herself became a trustee and after a meeting in the 30's it was reported in the *Long Trail News* that an increasing number of women were present, and "if this keeps up they'll be a majority and there's no telling what will happen!"

Other events were taking place as well, in particular the advent of the Appalachian Trail. With the Long Trail a reality, hikers wondered why long distance trails had to be confined to Vermont; why not a series of mountain paths that could take a wanderer across a whole region? J. P. Taylor had envisioned such a system when he first dreamed a day away on Stratton Mountain. It was Benton McKaye in 1921 of Sterling, Massachusetts, who first had the idea of a trail from Georgia to Maine along the spine of the Appalachian mountains. Work was begun the next year but it wasn't until the mid 20's that the Appalachian Trail system really got underway. Use of the lower part of the Long Trail naturally was a great help but not until 1925 did Dartmouth students, after three scouting trips, connect a trail from "English Mills," at Prosper, just north of Woodstock, to the Connecticut River and thence on to the Dartmouth Outing Club Trails and the Appalachian Mountain Club Trails in the White Mountains. In 1931 Willis Ross made the connection from Sherburne Pass to Prosper.

The birth of the Appalachian Trail

The Long Trail and the Club had grown up together through the first exciting years and now were learning to cope with the rather mundane task of maintaining miles of trails and upkeep of many shelters. In 1929 it was decided that the trail should be patrolled every spring to report on conditions and voted to equip a crew with axes and cross cut saws. They were to clear the trail from blow-downs, repaint blazes, and report to the proper sections the conditions of their part of the trail. But it was soon apparent that a spring crew wasn't enough, a summer-long patrol was needed, about $1,000 Mortimer Proctor estimated. It was the only way the Club could keep

1929 marked the advent of the Long Trail Patrol

the trail in the condition it was so proud of. "If the Long Trail isn't the longest, it's the best kept-up." The cost per day per worker of $3.50 was worth it.

Another mountain saint made his appearance at this time. Professor Roy O. Buchanan of the University of Vermont, famous for his thirty-six years of leading the Long Trail Patrol, for supervising the building of thirty-seven camps, notable designer of outhouses and, with his brother Bruce, the man who took the "almost" out of, "The trail is almost finished to the Canadian Border." Buchanan wrote, "we were tired of reading about that 'almost' . . . and we decided to take it out. After three days of bushwacking we came out at International Boundary Marker 592 and decided it would be a fitting end for the Long Trail." The Buchanan brothers were not able to do the actual job of cutting the blazed path, two young stalwarts, P. D. Carleton and C. G. Doll of the University of Vermont had that honor the summer of 1930.

Many are the stories of Roy Buchanan, cherished by young men who learned from him how one does things in the wilderness; how to judge the level of a cabin floor with a pan full of water, how to lay a trail

Roy Buchanan below, BHL, *and right,* *Phillips Carleton and* *Charles Doll.* GMC

up a steep slope; if tools laid on the ground start to slip downwards, cut a quick zig across the trail, or perhaps a zag. Professor Buchanan was a married man and although he had to be in the woods all summer he didn't want to be deprived of home comforts in the evening. In 1932 he fitted out the patrol truck with bunks, gasoline stove, pots and pans, and set off with his wife and young son to do battle with the wilderness.

Patrol Truck Number One had a personality of its own. A gift of Mortimer Proctor in 1929, this sturdy work horse was a familiar sight for twenty-five years, trundling along back roads, its porcupine-gnawed tires always on the point of collapse but faithfully carrying trail crews and their equipment. Its end was a fitting one when it was sold for $10.00 to a man in Rutland in 1954. There it finished its days in a backyard as a children's playhouse.

The Club is now on its third patrol truck; if the longevity of the other two is any indication this one should be around to at least 2020!

In October 1930 the *Long Trail News* proclaimed, "We are now able to announce the completion of the Long Trail to the Canadian Border!"

Patrol Truck #1 with Roy Buchanan on the running board. GMC

Post 592 marks the end of the Trail at the Canadian border. MF

"Just think of the layout now," wrote Theron Dean to C. P. Cooper, ". . . 260 miles of trail and some fifty cabins. You just wouldn't have visioned it could you, fifteen years ago? So harrah!"

It was time for a great celebration the Trustees decided, and celebrate they did. In September, 1931, three hundred members gathered at the Long Trail Lodge to hear greetings brought over the trail from the Governor of Massachusetts and from the Premier of Quebec. James P. Taylor spoke of the Club's 1,500 members, grown so miraculously from the original twenty-three; of the vigorous sections, the news letter and the guide book; the Long Trail Patrol and its Truck Number One, shelters and camps every five or six miles and best of all, 260 miles of well maintained trail. After a sumptuous dinner under the giant birchwood chandelier, the crowd moved outside. At 9:15 p.m., a gong was struck, President Mortimer Proctor lit a signal flare and up and down the spine of the Green Mountain Chain, fourteen flares on mountain tops were touched off, a spectacle seen as far away as Mt. Monadnock in New Hampshire.

It was after the Anniversary that it was decided the shelter terminology must be straightened out; just when was a camp not a lodge? The classification worked out as follows: a shelter was an open structure which could hold six people, a camp had windows, stove, table, benches, a wooden floor and could be closed. Sixteen people could enjoy a fireplace at a lodge which also had dishes and screened windows.

The Long Trail had become a reality. The Green Mountain Club was a thriving organization. It was well that this was so, for in 1933 a cloud on the horizon threatened the very existence of the Long Trail.

By 1933 the Great Depression had settled deeply over the country. Vermont summer resident William J. Wilgus, civil engineer and Vice-President of the New York Central Railroad, proposed that a parkway be built over the spine of the Green Mountains, much as the recently built Skyline Drive followed the southern Appalachians. The proposal was seen as a way to help Vermont's increasing

The famous yellow birch chandelier in the Long Trail Lodge's dining room. GMC

numbers of unemployed and as a means to bring more income into the state. Wilgus argued that it would fit into the Green Mountain Club's desire to get more people on the trail. They would do so, Wilgus said, if more could easily drive to it from a parkway beside the trail. A wave of approval followed. "Open up these green hills to the motoring public. Capitalize the hillsides from one end of the state to the other!" cried the *Burlington Clipper*. "It will present some of the finest examples of our northeastern scenery," claimed one enthusiast, "an artistic variation . . . much as we have in a great musical symphony!" The Trustees were not at all sure.

Mt. Ascutney in the early morning, from Pico Shelter. GMC Opposite; Col. Wilgus' proposed Green Mountain Parkway. BHL

At a special meeting in August, 1933 Col. Wilgus explained his plans. Much of the land for such a parkway, 1,000,000 acres, was already available said Wilgus. 100,000 acres had already been bought for a National Forest in the southern part of the state. There was Middlebury College's 30,000 acres known as the Battell Forest and the state's holdings of 16,000 on Camel's Hump, Mt. Mansfield and other peaks. Linked together they would make a right of way while the state would acquire a strip of 1,000 feet to make a parkway corridor. The project would employ 7,000 men with picks and shovels for a year and a half.

The roadway would follow the trail at a distance of a few miles, sometimes only a quarter of a mile

62

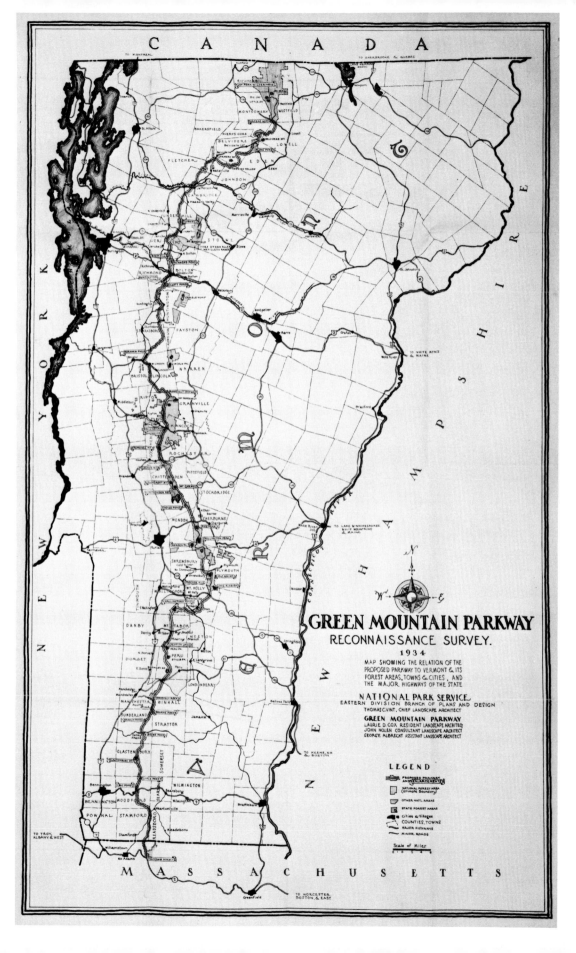

away and would be a hundred feet wide. There would be every effort to see that the trail would not be interfered with but he couldn't say just how often the road would actually cross the trail. And naturally, at especially dramatic spots, there would be vistas cut so that the cars could park off the road.

The trustees were appalled at what they had heard. "That our beautiful trail would be spoiled is, I think, beyond question. . ." said Acting-President Herbert Congdon. He was glad that the Appalachian Mountain Club had offered support but found that two of the Club greats, C. P. Cowles and J. P. Taylor actually favored the parkway (Taylor at this time was speaking from the viewpoint of the chairman of the State Chamber of Commerce, an organization he had pioneered much as he had the Long Trail), as did Mr. M. E. Wheeler, who gave the $100.00 seed money to start off the Long Trail on March 11, 1910, and who thought the parkway a splendid idea.

Congdon was also dismayed that some of the regular membership looked on the road as beneficial. Wasn't it unfair that only those who had the strength and endurance to climb should enjoy the unequalled scenic splendour? The unconvinced growled, "If people are too feeble to hike and wanted a mountain view, let them ride up Mansfield or Mt. Philo which had already been defiled by carriage roads!"

In spite of the stand of Taylor and Cowles, Congdon was able to muster enough support to issue a statement from the Trustees that the trail would lose

Jay Peak from the east, showing site of present ski area. VHS

interest for those who liked to hike and the Club having lost is *raison d'etre* would disintegrate. "The Green Mountain Club is unalterably opposed to the construction of such a highway."

Opinion, in the midst of the depression, was against the trustees and at a low point they dispiritedly agreed that probably the battle would be lost. Perhaps there was nothing they could do and had better accept the parkway with as good a grace as they could muster. "Maybe we can hike in the foothills," they said gloomily.

The battle raged for two years. Gradually opinion began to shift in opposition. One of the reasons was that the parkway as proposed would go from the Massachusetts line to Jay Peak with enough gas stations and hotels along the way so tourists would never have to leave the road and therefore would spend very little money in the towns. "Just a way to shunt visitors through the state into Canada."

Mortimer Proctor came back to take up his duties as President and to defend the Long Trail. He said that if the Parkway was built, "The great wilderness . . . still in large measure unspoiled by man would lose forever its charm of solitude."

In the end, after a bitter battle that more than once seemed lost, the Vermont House in 1935 voted against the Green Mountain Parkway, 126 against, 111 in favor. A state-wide referendum in 1936 killed

Post card view of Killington, left, and Pico in the 30s. GMC

65

it, although its ghost made a faint reappearance in the early 60's. Certainly the stand taken by the Club was of great help in preventing the blacktopping of the Green Mountains. In *Vermont History*, Frank Bryan and Kenneth Bruno conclude: ". . . that the most active interest group involved in the struggle was the famous Green Mountain Club . . . this group vigorously opposed the parkway. . ."

While the Club had been strong enough to take up a definite position against the parkway proposal, in the 1930's the Depression was taking its toll. Some of the 1,320 members found the $3.00 dues a luxury they couldn't afford; 111 in 1932 hadn't renewed their membership. The Club's pride and joy, the Long Trail Lodge, was operating under a deficit. Receipts for 1932 were off 40% from the previous year. Wasn't the Club managing the Lodge efficiently? Would professionals do it better? Reluctantly, the trustees decided to let the Treadway Hotel Company run the Lodge and under L. G. Treadway's watchful eye, use of the Lodge did increase, but membership continued to slip. Perhaps this was due to the inevitable draining-off of enthusiasm once the excitement of actually building the trail was over. Then, too, the saints of the trail were passing from the scene. C. P. Cooper and Fred Tucker were both bound for the Happy Hiking Ground where, as Raymond Torrey said, "Pack straps never cut, feet never blister, and where there is always cool water and shade." Raymond Torrey and Will Monroe were not far behind them.

The Trustees wondered if some of the hiking fraternity might be induced to join if only they knew of the healthful, inexpensive vacations that were to be had on the Long Trail for only 25 and 35 cents a day. A folder, "Short Trips on the Long Trail," was issued but what probably helped to attract people to the mountains and the Club was the advent of the skiing boom.

For years the vigorous men and women of the Green Mountain Club had been happy to tramp along snowy trails on snowshoes, taking time to examine animal and bird tracks, eating frozen sandwiches with relish and making overnight excursions to distant camps. Snowshoeing wasn't a pastime to attract everyone and there had been those folks who preferred

Treadway takes over as Pico becomes a downhill ski area

sliding downhill on enormously long skis. In the thir-
ties when the Norwegians and Austrians came over
with their new techniques and equipment, skiing
quickly attracted people who wanted a bit of speed
and excitement in their winter sport. In 1934 David
Dodge invented his endless rope tow. Woodstock
farmer Clinton Gilbert, whose cows were in the barn
in winter, didn't see why young Dodge couldn't ex-

*Snowshoe hike up
Laraway in the 30s.*

*Below; The Austrians
are coming! The new
style of skiing
perfectly demonstrated
on Pico. GMC*

periment with a rope and a model T engine on his pasture. If folks wanted to hang onto that rope so they could ski down again it was alright by him. Right on that little hill just beyond Woodstock was born the machine that changed Vermont.

It happened slowly of course. It was a novelty at first to slide instead of clumping through snow. Then the Boston and New York "snowtrains" began to bring city folk up on weekends to enjoy the northern wonderlands.

The Green Mountain Club oldtimers viewed all this with some apprehension. "It is doubtful if manufactured ski slopes permit the breadth of enjoyment known by Green Mountain Club members who still go into the mountains on snowshoes." Louis Puffer bewailed the lack of interest in snowshoes in preference for, "those long strips of expensive turned-up wood" but admitted that snowshoes weren't suited for "dashing down a steep slope at break-leg speed in order to have the pleasure of being towed back up by a power-driven cable." The main reason, Puffer said, for the "raquettes" demise was its lack of technical vocabulary. Snowshoers didn't sit around evenings discussing "christies, blitzies, and sitzies!"

A ski tourer in the 30s, lunching at Long Trail Camp on Pico with Killington in the distance. GMC

But the Club felt that it must move with the times with Pico right in its back yard. In 1936 Skiers Janet and Bradford Mead had begun to develop the west side of Pico Peak as a ski area with a tow. Treadway decided to keep the Lodge open all winter in an effort to attract the skiing crowd. Its walls were chinked and waterproofed and a furnace installed. Not surprisingly, it was found impossible to heat efficiently and in 1939 an annex was built across the road where the old Deer Leap Shelter had been. As an added inducement a half-mile trail was cut so one could ski right down to the Pico tow. The annex rates were certainly attractive; .75 cents for the night or $3.00 on the American plan.

Though no one knew it, skiing was here to stay. At the time there wasn't such a distinction between what today is called "cross-country" and "downhill". The boots and bindings of the era could be used

That new-fangled ski lift on Pico Peak, Feb. 1942 GMC

69

Skis firmly strapped to boots, the Austrian ski instructor ("bend ze knees, ten dollars please") does a show-off gelandesprung.
GMC

for either, and a skier who had spent the day on Pico's slope might be happy the next day to do a bit of touring. Accordingly, in 1942 Roy Buchanan and his crew were told to go ahead and widen the Long Trail, clear brush from old wood roads in order to link Pico with Pussin Kill Ski Area near Brandon. It was hoped, too, to extend the trail as far south as Bromley and north to Breadloaf; "Long Trail camps and small villages will provide ready-made facilities along the way."

It was an idea before its time. World War II prohibited any such expansion and when peace returned, downhill skiing, with increasingly sophisticated equipment, became a national craze.

Skiing had helped the Long Trail and the Club to survive the Great Depression, but the years of the Second World War took its toll. The *News* in 1944

70

said that, "in its 34th year of life the Green Mountain Club faces the most trying of times." Activities were drastically curtailed, maintenance of the trail and buildings were at an all time low. Hikers were off fighting around the world, membership was down but nostalgic letters from overseas, remembering the good old days on the trail, had members at home doing what they could to keep the trail in shape. The Patrol had been dissolved but faithful Roy Buchanan, now teaching all summer, spent what little time he had in trail work. There would be a lot of people using the trail when they came home, and the Club must not let them down. The Trustees pleaded, couldn't everyone do just a bit more in brush clearing and roof repairing? But it was difficult to recapture the do-it-yourself spirit of the early days, members had gotten used to having the Patrol do much of the heavy work and, besides, what could one do without gasoline?

Snorted veteran Willis Ross, "You'll have to do it just the same way we did it in the first place, get there any way you can and do it!'

Added to the Club's worries was the plight of its pride and joy, the Lodge and the Annex. At the height of the war the buildings had to be closed; with gas rationing in effect, they were operating at a loss, certainly no help in paying off the $25,000 borrowed to build the Annex. Things came to a head in 1944 when it was felt necessary to lease them to L. G. Treadway for five years. No one knew when the Lodge would re-open, but the burden of worrying about it and the Annex was shifted from the Trustees' shoulders for the moment.

When the war finally came to an end in May, 1945, the Long Trail was in bad shape. Blazes had faded, signs had disappeared, trails had overgrown. Carmel Camp, Cooley Glen Shelter, and the camp at Hazen's Notch had all fallen down and a number of others were so delapidated they would have to be replaced immediately. The sheet iron hut on Killington built in 1926 was in terrible shape. Many stoves in huts were on their last legs, windows were missing, roofs leaking. Lumber operations, south of Bennington and north of Camel's Hump, had to be cleaned up. "We owe it to the men to put the trail

The Long Trail deteriorates as hikers go off to war.

Post-war recovery posed many problems, blazes had faded, trails had overgrown

and its shelters in good condition . . . owe it to the club as well, for the reputation of the club depends very largely on the condition in which the hikers find the trails and camps. . .''

A year later in May 1946 the Club prepared for the first full hiking season since the start of the war by urging that all section trail chairman ascertain conditions of the trail and report to Roy Buchanan. If the shelters in a certain part of the trail were in poor condition the chairmen were supposed to post signs to that effect at the trail head.

In spite of hard work by the sections and individual workers the trails and buildings were still not up to pre-war conditions during the 1947 season; labor costs and materials were high and Roy Buchanan still hadn't had time to spare from his teaching to reactivate the Patrol. Finally, in 1948, the ancient Patrol Truck Number One, for years reported to be on its last tires, was to be seen once more headed for duty with its corps of husky young men under Roy's supervision. The Club breathed a collective sigh of relief!

There remained the troublesome problem of the Long Trail Lodge. Year after year had gone by and there was still no money coming into the Club's cof-

The first full hiking season since the start of the war

The famous old tin hut on Killington. Pico is in the background. PPM

fers from its operation and like Topsy, somehow the main building, the Annex and cabins and outbuildings had grown into a large establishment. There were complaints that members weren't patronizing it because its rates were too high.

It was time, too, to realize the hey-day of the country inn and lodge had passed; motels were taking their place. There was no doubt that the money resulting from the sale of the Lodge would be useful. For thirty years the Club had been proud of its property on Sherburne Pass, but in 1955 the trustees decided it was time to sell it. The Long Trail Lodge, favorite of three generations of hikers, passed out of the hands of the Green Mountain Club.

Thirteen years later, Vermonters opened their morning newspapers to read that the main building, the enchanted Lodge, had burned to the ground.

The Club had already had to deal with another piece of property, Will Monroe's beloved Couching Lion Farm, the Old Callahan Farm on the side of Camel's Hump. The peppery professor had retired there with his sister and a multitude of over-indulged

Deer Leap Cliff as seen from the roof of the Long Trail Lodge. GMC

73

dogs (no one ever dared to tell that to Will Monroe) making the farm a place of pilgrimage for mountain-lovers. When he died in 1939 he left it to the Club hoping the house and his library could be kept intact and used as a center for nature study. The main Club, already burdened with the problems of the Long Trail Lodge, could see no way to undertake Couching Lion Farm's upkeep nor could the New York Section raise enough money to take care of it. During the war years it was turned over with regret to the State to operate. Unfortunately they were difficult years to manage anything that required money or manpower, and the house and its gardens were left to return to the wilderness. Perhaps under the circumstances Will Monroe would have approved. Today he and his sister Katherine lie in a small cemetery surrounded by his dogs. Nearby is a ranger's cabin, made from the spruces planted by the Monroes and a parking space for those hiking the Forestry Trail.

Will Monroe and five of his best friends.
GMC

The Club had expected and hoped for a renewed interest in mountain hiking and indeed the men and women who dreamed of streams and woods while serving in jungles and deserts did turn to the Long Trail for solace and quiet. The war had brought some benefits to hikers; they could be seen swinging along under a Mountain Troop frame pack instead of the clumsy Adirondack pack baskets. Down-filled sleeping bags were available in army surplus stores, replacing the bulky pinned-together blankets of World War I vintage, while lightweight nesting aluminum kettles did away with the heavy frying pans. Even food was lighter; pliofilm bags took the place of waxed paper and mountain tents did much to save the shelter areas' spruces as did the newly developed mountain stoves.

New equipment makes hiking easier

But with the increased number of hikers came increased problems as the Trails and Shelters Committee was to find. Within ten years the Club was waging a desperate war to save the Long Trail System from an army of young folk inspired by the back-to-nature movement who were loving the trail to death.

It was the sheer increase in numbers of people on the trails, even considerate hikers, who were causing the problem. It was estimated that in one year, 150,000 people had set foot on some part of the Long Trail. As a result of this heavy impact favorite sites became blighted areas. Little Rock Pond Shelter, a place filled with magic for many who knew it, an island gem with a shelter that opened onto rocks sloping to a pond, was a paradise for three or four backpackers. When twenty tried to camp in or near the spot, it became a small hell. Shelter overcrowding became a fact of life during the 60's between the Massachusetts line and Sherburne Pass.

Increasing numbers of hikers bring serious problems to the Long Trail

Fragile, steep mountain trails turned into deep trenches, reported the Patrol, caused by fashionable heavy soled boots. And no longer did the tired hiker arrive at a sylvan campsite at the end of a long day but found instead a trampled area, denuded trees, a campfire ring filled with blackened cans and tinfoil. Inexperienced backpackers washed their pots upstream from the drinking area and the destructive emptied their rifles at the backhouse. On fragile mountaintops, campers ignorantly set their tents on clumps of

Little Rock Pond Shelter as it used to be. Opposite; Long Trail Patrol at work repairing the Trail near Molly Stark Shelter. Below; Group of young hikers, typical of the greatly increased numbers of people using the Long Trail. GMC

76

rare alpine plants that had taken years to grow. Vandalism had always occurred, but when word came that all ninety-two panes of glass had been broken at Cooper Lodge in 1962 it caused the Trustees to wonder if it was worthwhile bothering to replace them. It was obvious that something had to be done at once. The Green Mountain Club went to work with energy, imagination and ingenuity.

The first thing was to get the Trail itself back into shape. Under veteran Roy Buchanan the Long Trail Patrol found itself undertaking basic trail reconstruction in the most vulnerable and heavily used sections. Although the Long Trail was regarded as an "unimproved trail" it was now necessary to fashion permanent waterbars, place puncheons over wet places and install cribbing. The Trail was further safeguarded by discouraging spring hiking and actually closing the trails to Mt. Mansfield and Camel's Hump until they had a chance to dry out.

Litter reduction has lessened the blighted look afflicting many of the shelter areas with the advent of the backpacker stoves, light sleeping bags, easily prepared trail food in carry-out packages. Alas, the romance of a kettle of stew simmering over a camp-fire, spruce bough beds nearby is no more!

Combatting vandalism, educating thoughtless campers about camp etiquette and hygiene took a bit more doing. In 1969 the Burlington Section became so concerned about the misuse of Taft and Bolton Lodges under their care that the old system of caretakers was revived. It was not a new idea; in the 1930's it had been used on an informal basis. A Club member with a penchant for outdoor living might say to the trustees, "You know, I'd like to spend the sum-mer at Taft Lodge. I'll undertake to look out for it and the trails around it and make small repairs in return for a month or so on the mountain."

There had also been for a number of years official Caretakers at the old tin hut on Killington and at the camps on Camel's Hump. Now years later, it was ob-vious that the Caretaker system had to be reactivated. These days, twenty overnight areas along the Trail have Caretakers, male or female, acting as public rela-tions persons, educators, and doing nearby trail work. The fee for use of the area for overnight is $1.50 for non-members, 75¢ for members and worth every pen-ny! Caretakers have observed that many hikers these days come equipped with tents and the Caretakers are careful to assign tenting sites that have minimal im-pact on the area. With 2,101 overnight hikers in a fourteen weeks' period at Stratton Pond in 1974 it was obvious that the Green Mountain Club had a lot on its hands but that it was handling the problem well. And as always with the public there were times when one wished everybody would just go away and other times when one could not help grinning. Preston Bristow, Caretaker at Stratton Pond in 1974, remembers a tired man asking, "the sign at the road says this is the Long Trail into Stratton, but where is the short trail?"

While Caretakers solved many of the problems of over-use, sometimes more drastic measurers had to be taken. The shelter at Little Rock Pond, because of rapidly deteriorating conditions, had to be shifted

In days gone by, waste disposal wasn't much of a problem.
GMC

78

in 1972; other shelters too near trailheads have had to be moved to more remote areas. The "Adopt-A-Shelter" Program where one individual or a family keeps an eye on a chosen camp, making minor repairs and picking up, has helped to keep the Long Trail's reputation high and proved that the spirit of volunteerism is alive and well.

Disposal of wastes at overnight areas was the most serious in the whole range of problems posed by the hiking boom. The health of the people on the trail was at stake. Drinking safely from clear mountain streams has always been one of the attractions of mountain hiking. Until as late as 1967 it was still safe to do so. A relatively small number of hikers in the early days caused no trouble. Most of them were experienced in mountain travel. As the Club became aware of the increase in overnight campers at popular spots, garbage pits were dug and backhouses erected. They worked reasonably well until in the early 70's it was obvious something drastic had to be done, and quickly. The shelters and lodges near the tops of mountains were particularly liable to pollution, fly nuisance, and imperiled drinking water, for they were placed there to take advantage of the view. Rocky mountain ridges may be fine for looking out over the countryside but they lack topsoil to absorb wastes. The reputation of the Green Mountain Club as competent overseer of the Trail and its shelters was at stake. With the Appalachian Mountain Club and

Pollution, pollution, what's the solution?

"If you pack it in, pack it out," was the anti-littering message of the G M C. GMC

U.S. Forest Service the Club commenced working on a solution and in 1975 developed an ingenious method of handling privy waste at remote shelter sites. Bin composting, using principles of rapid aerobic decomposition, is now being used at seven sites on the Long Trail. "Overnight use during the five month 1983 hiking season at these seven sites was more than 3,200 people," writes Ben Davis, Northern Field Assistant for the Green Mountain Club, and one of those who helped to devise this method. "It has proven that composting is a viable waste management option in remote recreation areas." The word these days, says Ben, "is management, not disposal."

Bin-composting is a viable waste management option in remote recreation areas. GMC

Opposite; Hikers on an interesting climb on Mt. Mansfield's Forehead. GMC

There was another way in which the Club helped to protect the Trail; why not divert hikers to other, less well-known trails and mountains? With a never-ending stream of people all wanting to hike to the most popular places it occurred to Club President Bob Attenborough, in 1968, to start collecting information on trails on outlying mountains. The result in 1978 was a "Day Hiker's Guide to Vermont," now in its second edition and which thoroughly covers the state in seven sections.

In 1957 the Air Force handed the Club a bad scare. It had plans to install on Mt. Mansfield's Chin, a Bomarc Ground-Air transmitter. As it had done for the Parkway fight in 1933, the Club helped to organize an effective campaign in opposition to this threat with the invaluable help of Senators Aiken and Flan-

ders, Representatives Prouty and Governor Johnson. The Air Force in the face of such formidable opposition prudently decided that the transmitter could just as well be placed at nearby Fort Ethan Allen.

The Club had responded with ingenuity and hard work in dealing with the problems of overuse and the Air Force threat. Those were jobs that had to be done. It was the manner in which it acted to safe-guard the future of not only the Trail but the wildlands themselves that is one of the most praiseworthy efforts in the Club's history. By the late 60's it was apparent that the fragile ecosystems of Vermont's most popular mountains, Camel's Hump and Mt. Mansfield, could no longer withstand the impact of the hundreds of people who climbed their summits every day. A new summer-operated gondola on Mt. Mansfield, it was feared, would allow tourists to wander at will over the mountain top. Rare alpine tundra was disappearing, thin mountain soil eroding at an alarming rate. Mountainsides along the entire Green Mountain chain were being turned into ski villages, ski lifts were built on the very ridges along which the pioneers had blazed the Long Trail.

Over-use threatens mountain-top tundras as well as ecosystems

The "dusted-off" Skyline Parkway proposal of the Depression years coming back to life in the mid 60's alerted Green Mountaineers that they must act decisively. There were a number of members who were concerned that the only two instruments available to the state in order to protect land, the State Park and the State Forest, were not adequate. There had to be a better method of preserving land for its aesthetic value. Some sort of natural areas conservation legislation was needed. These members pursued such legislation through the Vermont Assembly and helped to preserve Camel's Hump.

At the same time, individuals living in the shadow of Camel's Hump who feared for the future of that unique mountain, the only underdeveloped major peak in the Green Mountain chain, began to plan strategy.

For its part the Club formed the Conservation Committee, whose purpose was to make Vermonters aware of their mountains as a natural resource.

In addition to these movements the Green Mountain Wildlands Profile Committee was set up to study the environment of the mountains. The Vice-Chairman was Dr. Vogelman of the University of Vermont, who had studied extensively the ecology of Camel's Hump.

The focus of these concerned individuals and committees fell naturally upon Camel's Hump whose distinctive bulk had not yet caught the eye of a developer. Together they worked out an effective campaign. People in the area drew up plans to protect their mountain while the Profile Committee warned of the dangers of disturbing areas above 2,500

feet. The Club endorsed the efforts of the concerned individuals and supported the Profile Committee both financially and with action. Under Chairman Shirley Strong the Conservation Committee outlined the philosophy of the Club's stand to maintain the wilderness aspect of the state-owned property. This stand was presented at many public hearings.

As a result of many dedicated individual's efforts and many long hours spent by Committee members, it was possible in the end to bring certain privately-owned areas into the state's hands. Today, Camel's Hump rises serenely above its green forests, a mountain belonging to all the people of Vermont. The Green Mountain Club is proud of its part in the effort.

Camel's Hump from the west. GMC

Restoration work goes on continually; Right, Gorham Lodge before repairs, and below, log replacement under way.

*Part of major
renovation of
Gorham in 1981.
Below, interior of Lodge
after renovation.
All photos GMC.*

The National Scenic
Trail System,
to join, or
not to join?

While protected mountains are one thing, protected trail corridors were another. It was amply
obvious by the 1960's that corridor protection was
needed in some form. The agreements worked out by
James Taylor and the other trail blazers in the early
days were adequate when Vermont's population was
shrinking, her hill farmers abandoning their hard won
mountainside acres, trees springing up again on
deserted pastures. Now Vermont's mountains were
under pressure, land was changing hands as the old
farm families sold off their holdings to city folk or
to big development corporations. Who owned what?
A landowners' committee was set up to find out, not
an easy task. Back in 1922 Willis Ross negotiated a
lease with an agent for a shelter in this fashion: "The
apple tree referred to is just south of your shelter and
on the trail, and I marked this tree with a pocketknife
with an hourglass in the bark for identification as that
was the only tool which I had with me at that time."

During this time the Federal Government began
to be concerned about the protection of long distance
trails and in 1969 President Johnson signed a bill im-
plementing a National Scenic Trail System. Did the
Club want the Long Trail to be included? The entire
length of the Appalachian Trail was, of course, in-
cluding that part of it which coincided with the Long
Trail from the Massachusetts line to Sherburne Pass.
But what of the northern half, the rest of the Long
Trail from the Pass to the Canadian Border? Did the
Club wish to hand over guardianship of the trail to
the National Trail System? The Club wanted time to
think about it.

As a spin-off from the campaign to save Camel's
Hump, the Club helped to put in place a unique program designed to save the fragile mountain tops.
Inspired by the recommendations of the Green Mountain Profile Committee the state set up a plan to station a number of specially trained rangers on the tops
of Mansfield and Camel's Hump, the two mountains
which received the most traffic. They were to guard
precious vegetation by warning hikers to keep to the
rocks on top, explain why this was important and in
general act as good ambassadors for the mountains
themselves. The plan worked beautifully but the
money ran out, and the program was dropped.

Alarmed that such a successful effort was to die, the Club offered to administer the program and provide a significant amount of the funds needed. Since 1975 it has had a contract with the Vermont Department of Forests and Parks to provide a program of public education, trail work, and information gathering. Now on a pleasant summer Sunday a hiker, scrambling up the last rocky yards to the summit of Camel's Hump or Mount Mansfield, will find him or herself greeted by a pleasant young Ranger-Naturalist. The conversation may be about the weather or trail conditions or about an unidentified bird, and the Ranger may break off to warn a youngster to walk on the rocks. An explanation of how old that tiny plant is and about the harsh environment in which it must live will, it is hoped, be a permanent lesson. That the program is working is shown by the fact that alpine vegetation is doing better and is re-establishing itself.

The Club is proud, too, that it is working in concert with three separate organizations to maintain the best possible conditions on Mount Mansfield; the Department of Forests and Parks, the University of Vermont, and the Mt. Mansfield Ski Corporation.

Sterling Section volunteers complete reconstruction of log bridge over Smith Brook below French Camp. GMC

Mountain tops have always been a magnet for hikers. Above is Camel's Hump from Dean Trail, GMC, and right, Professor Will Monroe and friends cross Burnt Rock. A Theron Dean slide. BHL

While the Green Mountain Club pondered the joining of the National Trail system, the Vermont General Assembly handed it a very welcome pat on the back. The Assembly had previously in 1960, on the Club's fiftieth Anniversary, adopted a resolution expressing its gratitude for the Club's role as the "founder, sponsor, defender, and protector," of the Long Trail System and delegated to the Club the responsibility for the "preservation, maintenance, and proper use of hiking trails for the benefit of the people of Vermont."

All members were pleased about this commendation but realized that with it came a charge of heavy responsibility. Would the Green Mountain Club in the future have the ability, worried the members, to deal with ever more sophisticated, complex, and demanding matters confronting the Club in its role as official guardian of the Long Trail System? Up until now the trustees, committee chairmen and volunteers, had wrestled with problems with skill and energy. Could an organization with members scattered from Montreal to New York City continue to administer the system properly? Or now, fifty years after that first meeting of enthusiastic amateurs in Burlington was it time to have a centralized office

Louis Borie took this picture of a young Ranger-Naturalist describing the fragility of rocky mountain tops.

with a salaried Executive Director? And what could be done to protect the Long Trail corridor from increasing encroachment of ski developments? Should the Long Trail north of Sherburne Pass be under the administration of the National Scenic Trail System?

The Club said "no" in 1975 to the last proposal. The National Scenic Trail protection was not for the Long Trail. The state agreed. Together they reasoned that in a time of greatly increasing numbers of hikers, inclusion of the Trail in a Federal Registry would only exacerbate an already difficult situation. In addition, it was felt that the Green Mountain Club and the state together were developing a measure of protection in their own fashion. And on balance the Club's record had been a good one — it would prefer to handle its own problems in its own way.

There remained the issue of a more efficient central control. Lula Tye, and later Minerva Hinchey, had been paid to handle the duties of corresponding secretary and treasurer and served the Club and the Long Trail faithfully for forty-five years. In 1977 conditions were very different from what they were when it was decided to pay Lula Tye for her work. Both the State and Federal Governments in the intervening years imposed increasing numbers of regulations on the wildlands in their protection. It was simply not possible to go into the woods and whack out a trail anymore. The Club had no choice but to take the step of hiring a full-time Executive Director. There was perhaps a sense of betrayal of the Mountain Saints, of the spirit of enthusiasm that characterized the heady days when C. P. Cooper set off with his axe to do battle with the wilderness, or when the Buchanan brothers vowed to take out that "almost." Nevertheless, dues were raised and a full-time director who was to hire, train, and supervise some forty summer employees and their activities was appointed. He was to buy supplies and equipment, assist with publications and most importantly deal with landowners and represent the Club with all Federal and State agencies. This was a far cry from the days when Taylor had to deal with the "Inker of Peru!"

In the following years it was inevitable that with increasing complexity of trail regulations and increased usage, two field supervisors had to be hired,

Headquarters moves to Montpelier and hires an Executive Director

one each for the north and south parts of the state. With the growing staff there was some concern that the volunteer spirit might fade. But the members, staff, and Directors have managed to work out a balanced "mix" of work that must be done to uphold the Long Trail's famous reputation. (The title of Trustee had been changed to that of Director).

The question of how to deal with ski area and real estate development continues to be a difficult one. In the days when James Taylor led his boys across the trackless mountains, Vermont was facing a far different problem from that of today. It was fighting the abandonment of hill farms, the continuing loss of population to cities and to other states. When Mrs. Alexandra Brown hiked the Long Trail south from Bread Loaf in 1925 to stay at Herb Haley's farm in Shrewsbury and liked it so much that she persuaded farmer Haley to sell it and its thousand acres to her (he was probably only too happy to do so), the Club rejoiced along with the state. Mrs. Brown's friends liked the area also and, said the *Long Trail News* with approval, "Now there is a sizable summer colony of people with means and taste located in the backwoods of Shrewsbury." It was to the

The third, and newest, Long Trail Patrol truck and a summer crew. GMC

Club's advantage to have such well-intentioned folk owning land along the Trail.

When in the mid 30's and 40's downhill skiing was just becoming popular, such activity, limited as it was then, was considered to be compatible with the intrinsic objectives of the Green Mountain Club and its Long Trail. Fifteen years later this notion proved untrue, the concept of a "Footpath in the Wilderness" was in trouble. Following World War II came the skiing boom and Vermont found itself an oasis amidst the megalopolis of the Eastern seaboard, an oasis made increasingly accessible by the interstate highway system.

The Club was concerned when in 1954 the state bought almost 2,000 acres on Jay Peak and wasn't entirely reassured by statements that at present there were no plans to develop it. Two years later the Sherburne Corporation surveyed a ski lift route on Mt. Killington. Next year came word that the Green Mountain National Forest approved of a plan to build ski trails and lifts on Lincoln Mountain. What about the fact that with wide ski trail crossings, hiking trails

*Ski trails on
Mt. Mansfield, courtesy
Vermont Travel Div.*

would be hard to find, and how about litter on a hitherto unspoiled mountain ridge, asked the Green Mountain Club? "Although the Trustees are not opposed to the advancement of organized skiing, we believe that certain areas of our national forest should remain in their mountain state as wilderness areas." At the same time Bromley and Mt. Snow were planning to enlarge, while Killington and Stratton were gearing up for large developments. It was not only that mountain-top restaurants and ski lift towers were sprouting along the Green Mountain Ridge, but huge real estate developments were beginning to be perched on the mountainsides as well. Today, the Long Trail is crossed by ten ski areas.

How to deal with the problem will be one of the Club's missions in the future. The other is corridor protection. With the help of an up-to-date list of landowners over whose property the trail runs, top priority will be given to the effort of assuring security for the route. Will it be feasible for the Club to reconsider

Jay Peak. The mountain top where the two figures are standing has vanished, blasted off to make room for a restaurant and the ski lift housing. PPM

93

the protection of the National Scenic Trail and National Recreation Trail Systems or will the Club continue to handle this problem as it has done in the past?

Despite real and very difficult problems good times continue to be the lot of Green Mountaineers. There have been exciting "foreign" expeditions, the first in 1978 to the Canadian Rockies, then to Great Britain, Yellowstone, and the Boundary waters. Such is the enthusiasm engendered by these trips that there are plans to mount one every other year.

There have even been some surprising events, such as the "re-discovery" of the cave at Sherburne Pass, and the birth of Fletcher Freeman Sewall who was born at Skyline cabin on September 6th, 1970. To mark the latter event, hitherto unknown in Club history, the Trustees voted to send the young hiker a ten dollar savings certificate!

The Club continues to work closely with the State and National Forest departments, and the sections faithfully see that their portion of the trail is maintained in the same good conditions as always.

The sections now number fourteen, the newest being the Ottauquechee Section, affectionately known to its members as the "O" Section, whose duty it is to care for the Appalachian Trail from Sherburne Pass to Prosper.

Members-at-large continue to play an important role in the Club, individuals who uphold the purposes of the Club but live too far away from organized sections to participate.

Intersectionals held at the end of the summer offer a week of hiking, talking and square dancing Trail friends who may not have seen each other for some time and, of course, new friendships are often made, as well.

Now a healthy seventy-five years old, the Club which began with twenty-three enthusiastic pioneers has over four thousand members, giving its full support to the ongoing struggle to preserve for future generations a beautiful but fragile part of our land.

The Long Trail continues to delight hikers who love the woods, streams and mountain peaks of Vermont, and the Green Mountain Club will see that this unique resource will remain, as it has from its beginning, "A Footpath in the Wilderness."

Opposite; The Footpath in the Wilderness still beckons hikers, as it did in the early days. VHS

Index

Photographs are indicated by bold-face numerals